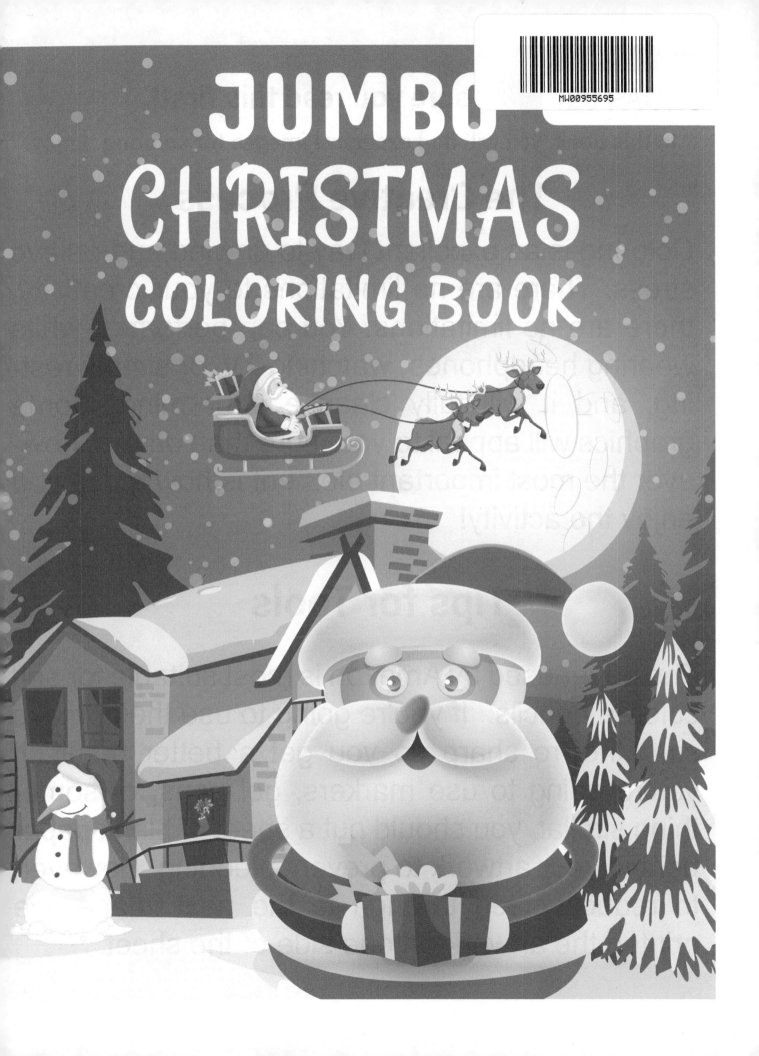

JUMBO
CHRISTMAS
COLORING BOOK

MW00955695

Make sure you read this first!

In this book, you will find exclusive images for coloring. Enjoy!

The Creative Process

Coloring is an excellent way to unwind and relieve stress. There are no limitations to your creativity; there are no limitations. You can perform it while wearing headphones, watching TV, or simply resting, and it will fully cleanse your mind. Some graphics will appeal to you more than others, however the most important element is how much you enjoy the activity!

Tips for Tools

The paper used by Amazon is most suitable for soft colored pencils. If you're going to use them, make sure they're sharp so you get a better result. If you're going to use markers, gel pens, or something similar, you should put a sheet of blank paper behind your artwork to prevent bleeding. However, to reduce bleed through to the next image, we printed the artwork on one side of the sheet.

Choose Your Colors

You will find a color test page at the beginning of the book. You can experiment with the colors on this page to see what works best. We recommend that you test the colors you wish to use every time because they can sometimes appear in a different way on paper than what you can expect.

Expertise

If you come across an image that you don't think is ideal for coloring right now, leave it alone; you can come back to it later! We recommend practicing every day because it helps you become more relaxed over time.

Sharing

Your talent is inspiring to see! I'd love to see your work!

We hope you will enjoy this coloring book.
We'd appreciate it if you consider supporting us with positive feedback on amazon.
We would highly appreciate it.

THIS BOOK

BELONGS TO

_____

_____

_____

Color Test Page

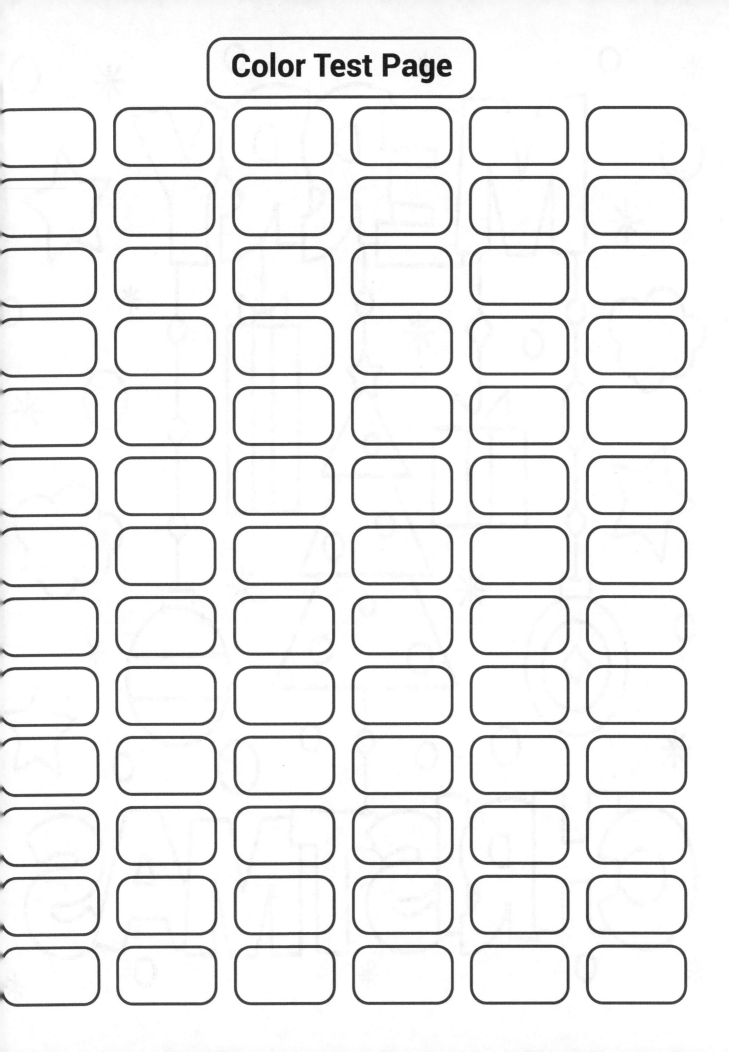

Made in United States
Cleveland, OH
03 December 2024

11280668R00070